Grace Period

PRINCETON SERIES
OF CONTEMPORARY POETS

OTHER BOOKS IN THE SERIES

Returning Your Call, by Leonard Nathan
Sadness And Happiness, by Robert Pinsky
Burn Down the Icons, by Grace Schulman
Reservations, by James Richardson
The Double Witness, by Ben Belitt
Night Talk and Other Poems, by Richard Pevear
Listeners at the Breathing Place, by Gary Miranda
The Power to Change Geography, by Diana Ó Hehir
An Explanation of America, by Robert Pinsky
Signs and Wonders, by Carl Dennis
Walking Four Ways in the Wind, by John Allman
Hybrids of Plants and of Ghosts, by Jorie Graham
Movable Islands, by Deborah Greger
Yellow Stars and Ice, by Susan Stewart
The Expectations of Light, by Pattiann Rogers
A Woman Under the Surface, by Alicia Ostriker
Visiting Rites, by Phyllis Janowitz
An Apology for Loving the Old Hymns, by Jordan Smith
Erosion, by Jorie Graham

Grace Period

Gary Miranda

PRINCETON UNIVERSITY PRESS

Princeton, New Jersey

Published by Princeton University Press, 41 William Street, Princeton, New Jersey
In the United Kingdom: Princeton University Press, Guildford, Surrey

Library of Congress Cataloging in Publication Data will be found on the last printed page of this book

Publication of this book has been aided by a grant from the Paul Mellon Fund of Princeton University Press

The book has been composed in Linotron Caledonia

Clothbound editions of Princeton University Press books are printed on acid-free paper, and binding materials are chosen for strength and durability. Paperbacks, while satisfactory for personal collections, are not usually suitable for library rebinding.

Printed in the United States of America by Princeton University Press, Princeton, New Jersey

FOR PATTY AND, LATER, FOR NICOLAS

Contents

Acknowledgments   ix

PART ONE / *VISIBILITIES*

Visibilities   5
   1. Fox   5
   2. Heron   7
Salmon Ladder at the Government Locks, Seattle   9
Still Lifes: Hoh Rain Forest   10
Magician   12
The Spider-Web Suns   13
Nocturne   15
Witnessing   17
The News From Moons   18
Where This Listening Could Go   19
The Animals of Where We Come From   21

PART TWO / *HUNGERS*

Hungers   25

PART THREE / *CONNECTIONS*

Connections   35
Deception Pass   38
Hood Canal: The Floating Bridge   39
Somewhere, Anywhere, Somewhere   40
Rough Draft for a Living Language   42
The Healing   43
The Gambler   44
Love Poem   46
A Marzipan for Einstein's Birthday   47
No One Is   48

Real Life   49
Like Myths   50
Narcissus   51

PART FOUR / *THE WORLD THAT IS OFFERED*

The World That Is Offered   55
   1. Even in the Dark   55
   2. The First Morning of Fathers   61
   3. The Noon of Everything   67

Acknowledgments

Some of the poems in this collection have previously appeared in various magazines, as follows:

The American Poetry Review: Part one of "Visibilities" (under the title "Field Trip"), "The Spider-Web Suns"

Argo: "The Animals of Where We Come From"

The Atlantic Monthly: "Witnessing," "The News From Moons," "Magician"

Poetry: "Salmon Ladder at the Government Locks, Seattle," "Still Lifes"

Poetry Northwest: "Deception Pass," "Somewhere, Anywhere, Somewhere," "The Gambler"

Salmagundi: Section two of "The World That Is Offered" (under the title "Clackamas River Suite")

Tar River Poetry: "Where This Listening Could Go"

"Hungers," "Visibilities," and "Love Poem" received awards from the Poetry Society of America in 1979, 1980, and 1981 respectively.

Grace Period

Part One / Visibilities

The sun doesn't like, um—doesn't like anything on it,
because it will make a lot of heat— 'specially a spider.
And the spider would, when the spider gets so mad . . .
um, I just know when the spider's on the sun he has
enough thread to wrap around the sun so it won't shine
any more. And I don't know about that, but I know
it happens.
—Tom Moscovitch, five years old, in an interview
about his drawings

Visibilities

1. Fox

Not one of them has seen it, but the fox
lives in the fields of these children's minds
as sure as real trees send roots their own size
into the balding earth. Say the word "fox"
and their eyes become dim windows that ancient
moths beat against from behind. Say "flower"
and they think "foxglove"; "song" and they sing:
"Oh the fox went out on a chilly night."

One of them, Leslie, a little older, says:
"We could get back to the school before it got us."
She's big on distances this year—the metric
system, her mother moving to another state.
It will do no good to tell her I was a child once
myself, or that foxes are the least of her worries.
All fear is equivocal. The only thing hers lacks
is accuracy, and when did content ever count?

"Maybe," I suggest, "we could get it to sit
for a portrait. You could all paint it."
"Foxes don't do that," Seth says—serious,
protective even, not telling me what they do do:
lurk behind bushes like gargoyles—lewd, toothy,
carnivorous—the strangers you don't take
candy from, their eyes terrible stars, burning,
their mouths foul with mucus . . . but why go on?

5

I think of those alphabet foxes—Disneyish-
cute and shy-eyed, not even sly. I think
of the leopards that pagan priests invited—
making them part of the ritual—into the temple.
The more I think, the more I like the fox
these kids concoct, that will strike like a match,
the blue-green of its eye adding an edge
to what we expect from fire, from foxes.

Soon enough their fox will become our fox.
But now, as they walk, the children tighten
their circle around me—an eye with its pupil,
frightened: Colin, the youngest, fingers
the tail of my jacket; Seth discusses weather;
Leslie looks up. Overhead, a jet trails
a thin line of vapor that widens and reddens.
The great eye of the sun burns in its socket.

2. Heron

Nearby there's a pond where a blue heron
constitutes news for the neighbors by his
appearances and disappearances. Apparitions,
I almost said. You'd think he's some dead
Gloucester fisherman, washed ashore, grown
graceful in the aftermath of fifty-odd
years handling nets while his fingers froze
and his beard matted solid with salt-spray.

They call him "blue"; he looks grey to me.
I've seen him only twice. Once through a tall
spray of cattails as I took a pee next to
the pond's edge. Another day as I drove by
and caught him in flight in my side mirror,
his legs dangling behind him, almost unwillingly,
the way you feel getting up from a chair
to do a chore you don't particularly want to.

Later, I learned that his mate, whom I've never
seen, was stoned by some kids on their way
home from school, fooling around, bored,
the same kids who skate on the pond in winter,
I suppose, making those swan-shaped S's on the ice.
The woman who told me never had children, I
could tell. The way her mouth curved down
when she said the word "kids" and her eyes flared,

I thought for a moment she was the bird
in question. "Herons mate for life," she said,

and if she was wrong, I hold that error high
among the precious few things I know about that
bird, or any bird. A poet I know—an ex-lover—
says you have to catch them out of the corner
of your eye—herons, I mean. She's probably right.
Still, I watch for this one whenever I drive by,

the same way I watch for meaning to move slightly
beneath the cover of everyday events, whose grace,
too, has an edge of sadness to it—not like swans,
imposing their cool will on any landscape,
but like herons, which always let us believe,
if we want to, that they might be something else—
a reed, a fleck of shadow changing shape in the wind,
a thought: the things we love, visible like that.

Salmon Ladder at the Government Locks, Seattle

FOR PAT THENELL

In an underground room, through windows
green with the thickness of glass and Shilshole
Bay, we watch the salmon pass, as though
their climb back to the rivers hinged on choice
and not the thin, clear message of the blood.

Teenagers, mothers with infants, anglers
who can't believe so many fish this size
could have eluded them through all those days
in August, teachers who know salmon lore
from social studies class, casual tourists—

what do we say to salmon, caught by surprise
on their turf, their eyes fixing us, those
dictionary definitions of eyes? How not seem
fatuous, vague, ingratiating, like telling
a famous artist how much you admire his work?

Our words, like our lures, would be lost
on these veteran lunkers that glide past,
grasping no thought but the one that reels them
in, their tails flicking froth, their silver
sides cross-hatched with survival. And still

we stand here, embarrassed almost, as if viewing
home movies of ourselves as children—no
soundtrack, just our lost, vulnerable bodies
come back to remind us: history, which watches
us move our lips, isn't paying attention.

9

Still Lifes: Hoh Rain Forest

In photographs of it you can hardly tell
which sides are up—a commentary both
on the nature of the place and on our compulsive
need to frame things simply, correctly.
The forest is right, I think, in its
refusal—though "forest" is too familiar
a word for what this place with its
hanging, or arching, greenery (like hairy
jump ropes captured at one apogee or
the other) does, or its nurse logs which say
to any comer: *Here—take root here!*

It's impossible to guess what—without
these paths, these plaques that assure us
not so much what grows, but that others have
been here—hard to guess what message such
hyperboles of verdure might convey.
Phosphorescent entrails. Spiny rafters.
Green gore of prehistoric spirits
spilt on our behalf (the timorous mind
insists "on our behalf"). The rain a fact
so close a man could live here for years
and not get wet, his toes curling like ferns.

As it is, though, curious tourists forage
for photographs beneath the drooping hammocks
of hemlock, fir, spruce, pine and an occasional

redwood, foreign here itself. Armed against
the wet in forest-green slickers mostly,
in spaced platoons of three or four, this
strange barrage of creatures files past,
pausing the briefest moment at each plaque
or for a snapshot, sensing the forest's
urge to turn us all to moss or lichen, Lot's
wife multiplied in jade, rainy forever.

Magician

What matters more than practice
is the fact that you, my audience,
are pulling for me, want me to pull
it off—this next sleight. Now
you see it. Something more than
whether I succeed's at stake.

This talk is called patter. This
is misdirection—how my left
hand shows you nothing's in it.
Nothing is. I count on your mistake
of caring. In my right hand your
undoing blooms like cancer.

But I've shown you that already—
empty. Most tricks are done
before you think they've started—you
who value space more than time.
The balls, the cards, the coins—they go
into the past, not into my pocket.

If I give you anything, be sure
it's not important. What I keep
keeps me alive—a truth on which
your interest hinges. We are like
lovers, if you will. Sometimes even
if you don't will. Now you don't.

The Spider-Web Suns

Reflections on a Child's Drawings

Everything is spiders or suns. Some
suns are spiders. Some spiders are webs
silhouetted against the sun, a partial
eclipse. The text is so full of spiders,
you forget, as you look at the drawings,
how few spiders really appear on the page,
or you don't see them: the sun's in your eyes.

Everything is poisonous—or, as he puts it,
"The poisonous is everywhere." It stings;
the spider stings; the sun stings the spider.
You think of "sting-ray," trying to make
the connection. You imagine he has, over
his bed, a webbed Japanese lantern
which, turned on, turns into the sun.

And yet, when he isn't drawing spider-
web suns, he seems just an ordinary
child, a small person who counters your
big-person questions with sound logic.
"It's cork—do you know where cork comes from?"
He thinks about this for awhile, then says:
"It can come from bottles." You know he's right.

You know, too, that his spiders will soon
diminish, his webs unspin, his suns
go down, all of them saved, perhaps, in his

mother's closet and in your own memory,
which—eclectic, unpredictable—will conjure
these images up in a flash some night
when your courage fails, or your marriage, and

knowing, announce: "Oh. *That* sun. *That* spider."

Nocturne

More like a bear than a cat, the creature
stood on the floodlighted back lawn
and watched what I would do. And when,

after mirroring his eyes for some seconds,
I took one footstep toward him, he turned
and walked toward the bushes, determined

to seem calm—like an adverb, or like a man
who has an important meeting to get to and,
since he's already going as fast as he can

within the bounds of dignity, does not glance
at his watch. To watch anything move with grace
away, and knowing how things have a tendency

not to return, is to feel the twine of the stomach
unwind in that direction. Suppose I had spoken
to him in a language we both, with a little luck

and patience, might have understood. Surely
my own fear was foolish—that if he had really
gotten to know me he would have, eventually,

been disappointed. And if in my fear I imagined
his heart beating against his ribs like a luna
moth against a window, did I betray the legends

that lay behind his terrible eyes?—terrible only
to me perhaps, like the eyes of those salmon
that used to flop in the boat bottom even

after I had hit them so many times already
with the pliers I would have sworn they were dead.
The underbrush, when he entered it, said

"large," said "not domestic." I stood on the lawn
listening for further instructions, but none
came. I said to myself: "Raccoon . . . raccoon."

All that night, I kept the floodlight on.

Witnessing

FOR PATTY

Beneath leaves of a plant that's named for milk,
that bleeds milk, we search for chrysalides—
things that I've never seen, but whose name I like.
And I think, as I look, of all the things

you've taught me to name—larkspur, loose-
strife, sea lavender, plants called hens
and chickens, butter and eggs, your eyes
bright with such knowledge, as solid as nouns.

Just so, you tell me now of creatures
who choose the underbelly of these leaves to make
wombs of, studded with gold, from which emerge
monarchs that range the length of the Atlantic

in hordes—one more fact I must have missed
by skipping the fourth grade. And when, today,
we find no trace of anything resembling this
miracle you mention, and I'm about to say

you made it up, you bend down, break a pod,
and blow unlikely butterflies in the sky's face—
not black and orange like monarchs, but cloud-
thought white, or like the way I mark my place

when I read your eyes, which, witnessing, claim:
This is the world. Try to learn its name.

The News From Moons

Jupiter has eleven, or nine—I don't know
which, or whether they resemble ours
or even each other. A moon is a moon.
Perhaps. But, science aside, we shouldn't
underestimate the mystique an eye
lends to any landscape, mistaken or not.
And the eye is connected somewhere—just as the ear,
caressed, has lines like a telegraph to the shuddering
loins, except the eye's connection is less
predictable, more varied, and to a place
not charted on anatomical maps.
I have seen maps of the moon even—ours,
I mean—where every bump and indentation's
labeled: Grimaldi, Landsberg, Rabbi Levi—
names no moon would think of giving its children.
What we call a thing should matter. A moon
would come, called by its true name, as when
the eye beckons from that place: *Here, moon . . .
here, moon*—though not in so many words. A moon
has as many names as the eye can give it, and knows
them all, and can't be fooled. Moonagamy
is fine, but think if we had nine or eleven
moons flashing their bright news—like plankton
when you splash in the sea at night, or a good day
on Wall Street—such a cache of news each eye
would need a college education, and have
to specialize. . . . On second thought, I think
I'll take our one the way it is, that
flat white stone in the sky. Skip it.

Where This Listening Could Go

FOR JOYCE COHEN

There was hardly a shed where this listening could go,
a rough shelter put up out of brushy longings,
with an entrance gate whose poles were wobbly. . . .
—Rilke, Sonnets to Orpheus

They call it Colin's Gateway. Standing there,
you can see the whole of Asia pouring like salt
into the Adriatic. Some mistake it for the letter
A, a small house, and are only partly wrong.

Where it leads is everybody's guess, but I
have moved through it to a country where round
trees interlock like those circles you make
in Penmanship, and where you can ride their tops

like a winged creature, who, used to wings,
prefers to slide down grey curves into crevices
and climb the lacy branches again—an angel
doing a fair imitation of a child—and where

carpenters show you the real meaning of wood,
planed to a finish smooth as amber. If you can,
go there in the rain, or when clouds are performing
a symphony by Haydn. Grey is its best color,

moving—with the speed and slight smile of the sloth—
into white. Its fondest hope is to become light,
not the light an object catches, but that which
it gives off—as if, Heraclitus aside, you could

actually see light and dark in themselves rather
than as gradations of shade or even as qualities
known by their opposites. In such a land, no one
would think of husking words of their meaning

or turning voices upside down and shaking them
till the mind could hear only what it wanted
to hear. The voices there are gravelly with
bright pebbles, the masculine counterparts

of rivers—voices that have no credence in our
world except in our dreams, where what matters
is what happens and is its own justification;
or under water, where music issues from deeper

instruments than breath can set in motion,
as if notes vibrated from sheer color or the sway
of sea grass. They are melody revised, turned
inside out, as hard to describe as the month

after December—not January over again, but
a lifting off the runway of what we call a year
into some brighter season, announcing, at the end
of it, new synonyms for what we need to know.

The Animals of Where We Come From

(Cain speaks)

The borders of that country are guarded
by costumed animals who keep their
backs to me always—wolves, I think,
though their tails, if they have tails,
are tucked beneath the grey greatcoats
of their kind, and they wear fur hats—
wolf-fur, now that I notice, which surely
precludes their being wolves, or insures it.

What does any crime become, looked at
askance years later, the way we catch sight
of insects in tall grass and only then notice
their incessant whirring? Our earlier selves
are always saintly by contrast, creatures
of transcendent ignorance who deserved more love
than they got. Thinking of them, we are wolves
chewing our own legs loose from our own traps.

And if I did murder my only brother—not
that I remember or admit it—because his
gifts were more acceptable, I do not say
my act was right or wrong, but only that
a slim hinge holds the door of what we call
convention, and the animals of where we come from
hunker there, hungry, a knowledge of extinction
burning like a furnace in their eyes.

Part Two / Hungers

Have they seen, ever, the sharp bones of the poor?
Or known, once, the soul's authentic hunger,
Those cat-like immaculate creatures
For whom the world works?
—Theodore Roethke

Hungers

FOR JANNA SMITH

1.

A disease of the heart. You cannot catch it
from cats, or from sitting too long in a draft
after a shower. The heart complains: "Begin,"
or "Stop," or "To hell with all this talking,
let's make love." At times the heart does

perfect imitations of the bowel, which it prefers
to call the stomach, saying: "A man cannot
out of the troubled stomach draw such art
as will preserve him. Believing himself not
loved he cannot, no, at least by someone,

retrieve such songs as will into the dark
of other men send light." The heart really
talks like this, and gets away with it.
The mouth says things like "Yes, I'm hungry,"
or "The least you could have done was kiss me

goodbye." It is hard to like the mouth,
that liar, confusing as it does the symbol
for the substance. Better, perhaps, to say
nothing, but go for the eyes, those sad circles
in the face of "goodbye" that watch the words

stretch out toward their next full stop. Or,
better yet, the throat, whose growls are at least
sincere. Better to let your hands have their say,
not listening at all as the heart tries hard
to undo the first morning you were not a child.

25

2.

Nothing ever happens, the beaten prisoner
thinks as his nose flattens against his cheek
like a hinge or the lid of a sewing basket
or anything which, sadly, does what it does.
The boa tightens its grip imperceptibly

and the mouse inhales less and less with each
breath till nothing is left of air. The hyena
eats alive, still on the run, the wildebeest,
snapping and tearing the flesh with its steel-trap
jaws till the bowels trail in the yellow dust

and the wildebeest falls like a tent collapsing.
We die, someone has said, from our whole lives,
the dailiness of things. Bright angels caught
in the armhairs of God, spirals of wingbeat,
we long for the solidity of wood, the hunger

of fire, though we know the latter burns the former
till the ashes pile up and need to be swept out.
We are those ashes, though we cannot remember
having been that wood, that fire. We pass
each other truths like salt which says:

"This product does not contain iodine,
a necessary nutrient." It doesn't contain
a lot of things we could mention, but what
container would be large enough to list
them all and still be small enough to lift?

3.

Seasonal as salt, a mean-spirited time
consumes us all. Where does the heart
begin? If the foliage disappoints,
is it not indicative of the eye's failure
to become excited? Does the maple's

iridescence bore the sky? The aspen,
with its "rainy-sounding silver leaves"
stirs a place that cancels checks,
schedules, easy answers. Miracles
blossom in all our eyes, which, opened,

watch them flap into a sky too blue
to be questioned. We clear our throats
and turn back to "the dailiness of things,"
wanting to be stroked down, wanting
ourselves to be lifted off into that

(the heart might say) cerulean span.
Such instances are fast becoming extinct,
and the lines we wind around our dear-held
images of ourselves will soon wear out,
not bear, at least, repeating in a way

that we ourselves can credit. Call it
"blight." Not a sad word. A shimmering
unto death, a depletion of spirit.
There are more rifts in the universe
than any love of ours will ever cure.

27

4.

What weather plies its art on the platitudinous
air today? What reason, for that matter,
for getting out of bed? The mailman comes?
The onions mildew in the cellar, and someone
should be told? The sea has the hiccups,

and you are the only one with a bag big enough
to help, a face scary enough? Without even
looking out, you know the sky radiates some
ineluctable message about the total scheme
of things. Either that or total indifference.

Whole continents drift beneath its ample
brooding. And yet how sad not to have color—
let alone to see it—but always to be
a source to others, an ethereal reference,
marginalia for sun, planets, moon, stars.

Just so, we have this space between us,
to keep the colors of our mistakes
from running into one *en masse* conclusion:
black. We have these minutes—millions
of them—that must be taken seriously,

and will not easily lend themselves to love.
To be alone, and still to believe you exist,
is a major thing. I have seen bougainvillea—
I think in Brazil—vermilion against the sky,
and have known that this, too, is important.

5.

At the synapse of certain moments many
beautiful things happen. The mind holds
their textures up to the light and lets them
fall, some forming themselves into meaningful
patterns, some scattering like confetti.

It almost seems as if God were playing
kick-the-can with the world, or that whole
eons of birds were evolving backward to fish,
then cells, then nothing, but a nothing that
throbbed with the nerve-endings of everything.

Those spiky remnants of volcanoes
that we stub our toes on daily, thinking
"Who the hell left that there?" Or the sparse,
incipient nudges toward belief we brush
away like dandruff or mosquitos. Pesky

things. Unmanageable too, for serious souls
intent on intention. But there are times
when they take on the huge, exclusive importance
of certain insects, the stamen of a flower
viewed through a microscope, as if our inner eye

froze on the frame called "now." Compared to such
moments, our saner insights seem the natural
consequence of blatantly poor research, thought-
problems in math we didn't solve fast enough,
and whose numbers, like so many marbles, roll away.

6.

If men and women grew fat on wisdom, we
would all be starving faster than we are.
The eyes of children in India are black
coins that they give you for money, whether
you give them money or not. The mothers

rub the hands of infants across your hands,
your arms, until your hands your arms go numb,
the insides pricked with the blue striations
of ice. Whatever unhappens there will happen
again. Whatever you do, the scaffolding

of your deeds will totter beneath such hungers,
which are your own. Make, if you want,
the syllables dance, the consonants lean
toward each other like lovers in a café
crowded with vowels. Like everyone, you

are partly wrong. Threading the eye of the next
moment with the thread of this one, the world
happens. At times, nobility. The raw material
for lives unwavering as rock. Meanwhile, meaning
ravels at the edges, grumbling: "Victory, Defeat."

We lie down under the dark forgetting and wake
once more to birds intent on their own business
of being. Before we remember our names we can feel
the worms of doubt gnawing away at our dreams.
But the body, nobody's fool, puts on its shoes.

7.

Between the dreams and the shoes we try
to deserve our deaths, to loosen the knots
that bind us to earth, time sucking its breath
in. If our hungers lean toward heaven—and
they seem to sometimes—it is either an illusion

we cannot afford to trust, or a fact better
left in the realm of partial inattention, like
grocery prices. We must get on with our lives,
which are all of a piece if we could only make
the connections. Sometimes it is a person—

Lou Andreas Salome, who linked Rilke, Nietzsche,
and Freud in a trinity more terrible than God's.
Or dates which, thought about, astound:
that Frost was seventeen when Whitman died.
On any map the great cities tug at our eyes,

but there are those intersections, countless,
where the rest of us, who have our flashes,
hold things together. Even as you brush
your teeth, a hurricane rehearses its own
version of tranquility; in some unprecedented

north an ice floe twitches in its sleep. These
images move when you move, *because* you move.
That face in the mirror—did it turn away
when your face turned away? If you look
back now, your life may never surprise you.

Part Three / Connections

Connections

The steam spurts out from under
the iron like little shouts for help.
Mother thinks I'm asleep. I like
how she makes the iron hit the clothes
with a solid whack, the way Daddy
hammers a nail. I'd like to make
something hit something that way,
like I was putting my name on it so
tight no one could get it off.
But it's sad too—not for the clothes,
but for Mother. You can tell
it's not a job she's going to get
done—not in her head—even if
there were no clothes, or people
stopped wearing them. The clothes
wear her out. People wear out clothes.
How strange! And it all comes
from the wall, up through that cord
to the iron that connects Mother
to the iron and the iron to my
blouse. From the wall. Like mice.

If I keep my eyes half-closed
like this, I can watch and Mother
doesn't know, like I was looking
from behind a waterfall. It's nice,
but scary too. I can tell Mother
isn't connected to me the way
she would be if she knew, the way

the iron's connected to the wall.
I don't like to think how things
unplug and then no juice can go
through. It's sad. But with Mother
and me now, it's like—like we're two
ladies here, like I was one of Mother's
friends who goes back to her own
house when they're through talking.
And there *is* no juice between houses,
except for telephone wires, but it's
not the same. It isn't juice,
I don't think—the telephone—not
in the wall so you can use it, like
for the iron. It's something colder.

I wonder why my blouse doesn't try
to get away, the way oatmeal jumps up
when it gets too hot, and bacon
stands on tiptoe so that not too much
of it touches the pan. And popcorn.
I guess the iron must hold it down.
I used to think. . . . What did I
used to think? I wouldn't have
pretended to be asleep back then,
though I don't know why. I was smart
enough to think of it, I just wouldn't
have done it. What did it mean then
that it doesn't mean now? Now
I feel more like an iron that doesn't
need to be plugged in—like it ran

on batteries, except I don't think
they make them that way. Strange.
Everything is so strange today.
Like: I'm here, my mother is there,
and all around us there's this
house. And it's just—a *house*.

Deception Pass

If brothers happen to forget each other,
do they dissolve, evaporate, or just thin
out to something they'll have to find another
name for—the way fog is a name for tall rain
left standing after the grazing season?

Once, near Deception Pass, in a dense
fog the salmon had tricked us into (leaping
always too far ahead of the boat), our eyes
became like those dots in the Sunday paper
puzzle page, where, even without a pencil,

you get the picture. The things brothers
don't tell each other can smell blood a mile
off, and such silence, hooked in their mouths,
can hurt, whichever way they turn. All
men are brothers—or, at least, that truth

is a fog the world likes to get lost in. But
brothers know better: no distances are
as real as the closeness which separates
them. I've lived apart from mine twenty-four
years this year. We phone to celebrate

birthdays—a morbid kind of keeping score.
I go back home whenever I can: we talk,
joke, go fishing. And yet. . . . Forging
upstream toward their first home, Chinook
salmon age in two weeks those twenty-four

years our time. Some of them die, trying.

Hood Canal: The Floating Bridge

A canal says to the land: *you go here,*
you there. Lovingly. And the land goes.
And the water goes to sleep. And the people
of that place contrive ways of getting
from here to there without waking
the water. Such is the "problem" of water.

A floating bridge does not resolve that problem.
It embraces it. Such is its way of loving,
a respect, a refusal to interpret the water's
dreams. To such a bridge the land lets go easily,
as a mountain to its foothills, or a man's spine
to the sperm's need to leave—that is, to return.

Or so it seems. And yet, attentive, one can feel
the water deepen beneath the bridge, darken,
and plot a resolve. The water will not be loved,
not like a dog or a simple wife. The water
will offer its love to those who have not
deserved it. Such is the nature of water.

When the winds came, when the cars cowered,
when the bridgekeeper stripped himself of his title
as if shedding a useless skin, when the water's
dream broke loose of its moorings, becoming what
it had always meant—not what it said—the bridge,
like a cogent argument for temperance, collapsed.

And the distance between here and there
entered again the vocabulary of that place.

39

Somewhere, Anywhere, Somewhere

1.

To start somewhere. Chrysalides in summer
unhinging their wings. A pheasant cock
exploding. A light breeze and the hornets,
like uncooperative kites, slapdashing
against your clothes. It is right

to hold this moment against the next one,
light as skin, the kiss before the kiss.
June, July, August. An armada of wildflowers
nudging things on. A single car on a dirt
road, raising dust. A beer can spurting open.

2.

Anywhere. But not the planned itinerary,
not Jason with a calculator, Medea
checking her recipe for children. If you
have lived on this planet thirty years
you know as much as the next person:

the scissors action of gain and loss; small
graces which, ignored, grew like Pinocchio's
nose. Given the stars on a clear night,
everything is a lie: the trick is
to choose the one that matters most.

3.

In the sun, to get an even tan, turn over.
Some truths outstrip the mind's elastic
urge to synthesize, to wield a wedgy
hammer between one fact and the next.
St. Lawrence, on the gridiron, said:

"I'm done on this side"—the only martyr
besides St. Thomas More who had a sense
of humor. Somewhere, as you read these
lines, a young woman is letting go of
her childhood, that kite, that butterfly.

Rough Draft for a Living Language

First of all, we will have to eliminate
useless phrases. "Needless to say,"
should be the first to go. Then, "If I
were you"—as if you weren't, or wouldn't
do exactly what I'm doing if you were,
so why bother? Everyone's everyone.

Secondly, we will have to increase
the distance between the words, so that
listening might enter our active
vocabulary. This precludes, of course,
present telephone rates or operators insisting
your three minutes are up. Nothing is simple.

Next, we will have to learn again
to remember—not in code, as we do
now, or simply as reflex action, but
passionately, knowing that words are
events, invisible, and will not survive
if put in cages. Not for long.

Finally, we will have to teach ourselves
the long patience of the not-born, slow
as the eye's perception of exploding stars
seen from a distance no one has ever
traveled, or everyone has but doesn't
remember, or hasn't the patience to tell us,

knowing, needless to say, we aren't listening.

The Healing

The season wounds like a stone. Kites
waver in the wind, but only as a prelude
to finding their true centers. Or call it
"learning to fly," as though wind instruments
had it all over the strings. The latter require
practice on a scale unthought of by amateurs
or dabblers in statistical improvements.

As for the space around that wound
it is amethyst and of a weight not measured
by instruments, wind, or string. In physics
waves are illustrated by strings, remember,
but wind waves are direct and speak their own
names to those who listen. You are still that
audience if you just believe it loud enough.

But take a concrete example: a swan
at Craigsville Beach—in a pond there—dives
and dives, its black legs ambivalent and awkward,
its grace diminished to a need more potent
than the need to impress—either us or some
other swan. Later, landing in water, it will
sound its unswerving noise loud enough.

Even the beauty we lose has an edge
of gain, is what I mean to say. Or, as Rilke
says, the earth in spring is like a child
who has memorized difficult poems, so many
poems, and who gets the prize. What the season
needs will happen, though the pain is real
enough, and ours, and even the healing hurts.

The Gambler

Say there's a Muse of money.
Or that plastic chips beat paper
bills hands-down as collateral
for actual grace. There's a back
room in the brain where lamp-
shades dangle and the odds
get better, the more you lose,
that you'll leave a winner.
Meanwhile, in the corner, a teletype
keeps pumping news that somebody
up there likes you.
                          You believe it.

In some cases, that place invades
the body: going up for a jump-
shot; the long moment before you
come. Casinos are only analogues
of anatomy. However often
you lose, there's always an exit
sign that reads: "Tomorrow: to be
continued." Money comes from
somewhere, like the sun. Inside
you're still your mother's son,
a favorite.
                    You like long shots.

Not that any amount of luck
will slake your thirst. Toward
evening there's that restless hour
you're sure the world is out there,

winning without you. If you
marry, women multiply—a parley
you know you should have played.
Everyone's laying odds you'll never
have your cake and eat it. What
do they mean, "have"? You see their
bet, you raise the cake.
                                  You eat it.

Love Poem

A kind of slant: the way a ball will glance
off the end of a bat when you swing for the fence
and miss—that is, if you could watch that once,
up close and in slow motion; or the chance
meanings, not even remotely intended, that dance
at the edge of words, like sparks. Bats bounce
just so off the edges of the dark at a moment's
notice, as swallows do off sunlight. Slants

like these have something to do with why *angle*
is one of my favorite words, whenever it chances
to be a verb; and with why the music I single
out tonight—eighteenth-century dances—
made me think just now of you untangling
blueberries, carefully, from their dense branches.

A Marzipan for Einstein's Birthday

As rain sometimes against the rock
of a singular thought effects its own
undoing, turning from drop to plop
to wet, which, caught by the late-
arriving sun, shimmers in the after-
thought of easy money, so do the words
of the great dissolve in the mouths of fools.

In spite of this, the majesty of rain
is sheer largesse, if only by default—
that is, a code that can't be broken,
though the shapes of clouds are
corrigible enough, and lightning,
however oracular, is merely a glib
god's version of instant hype.

The space between the world and any word
is rife with political static, statistical
strife, and the census confirms not
every sail that swells with breeze
is big with child. In short, by the time
two people know a truth, it isn't
true. Given which, I side with those

conspiratorial spirits that arch, like
invisible rainbows, somewhere beyond our
repertoire of medicinal music. Big
with fable, they strike like constel-
lations the mind's eye, a blight
on philosophies you or I might salvage
or savor, stranded, high and dry.

No One Is

No one is

what his best thought says he is.
Too much depends on the careless moment—
a hatchet's haphazard kiss, eyes without
body or warning staring down the headlights.
The neck can snap so quickly even dreams
can forget to file a change-of-address
card. Fingers can leave hands, and how
can either of them wave goodbye?
        *
In a small grotto of grapeleaves
on a porch a single spider lives
in whatever anonymity he can sustain.
Sooner or later the noisy children
find him, the school bus late, the wind
forcing them back off the road
into a trellised grotto. Such
patience . . . such pointless bravado.
        *
A flick of anger like a snake's tongue
strikes. The wound is unforgiving.
Later, editorials will stir the bland
community to a rage akin to sleep.
In their polyester dreams, the wives
will grind bones to a fine dust:
no one is going to get off easy.

No one is.

Real Life

What interested me was the wingbeat of doubt
I detected in the gut of the playground
bully, fluttering like the tiny dot
on a TV screen, but never quite going out.
Something in me recognized that sound,
though I had mastered the less-than-martial art
of striking love, not fear, into the hearts
of teachers, not of students—mostly nuns.

He heard it too in me—a common secret.
When I made wisecracks under my breath
in class, he'd broadcast them and get
the credit: laughter, the teacher's wrath.
We had a pact: the old trick of split-
ting up, like cowboys taking different paths
to see which one the posse would go after,
which one would survive. We'd meet later.

They went after him, of course, and we didn't
meet. The last I saw of him was Father
Mack in class slapping his face livid
for cheating, then shoving him out the door.
I don't think of him often, but whenever
I do I always think of the phrase "real life"—
that is, some tougher part of town, a kid
you knew you couldn't play with and survive.

Like Myths

Far below this plane a cloud
extends like a huge brain
pressed flat, but not quite flat.

The shadow of the plane's a passing
thought, a grey spot on the cloud's
good day. We who are in the plane

are in the shadow too, even though
the shadow has no windows as the plane
has. Inside the shadow, we cannot

see the plane above us (where we are
as well) or know we cast a plane
against the sun. Within its thought

of shadow the cloud is thinking us.
If we—here—should fall, the plane
would cross the cloud's mind—a different

thought from shadow, or from us.
Meeting ourselves in shadow, we would
die like myths—hard—before we died.

Narcissus

I have always known this: my being
was an excessive gloss on my own
attempt to communicate, a wheel
on which a dream of wheels spun.
Arbitrators came, mute companions,
watery gods. Their silence bred
alternatives I could not condone.
The moon rose like a handmirror, black
as its input—not a moon at all,
now that I reflect. The space it
didn't take became my name for it—
"night"—a reversible coat the day
believed in and put on. Later,
in the swerving sentence of my longest
thought, my own body drifted down-
stream, face up, factual as song.
And as the poem—even the word—
is a fracturing of one will into two
so that the two may contemplate each
other with benign hostility, like two
magnets with their backs turned,
existing only in their mutual exclu-
siveness, holding each other at a distance
again and again, so did I become
what I gazed upon and loved—that is,
myself, flowering into the world.

Part Four / The World That Is Offered

The baby isn't late really; this is just a grace period.
—Patty, nine months and two weeks pregnant

The World That Is Offered

FOR NICOLAS

I. Even in the Dark

1.

Tonight, outside my window, a mockingbird
runs through his list, his repertoire of twitters,
chorts, glissandos and olés. I listen
but lose count, and my one-year son, immune
to impresarios, sleeps right through it.
The mockingbird could be his patron saint,
for, like the bird, his gift for imitation
makes me smile, even in the dark.

I hear him sometimes, mornings, in his crib
performing small etudes. He pats his toys
for counterpoint: *piano, pianissimo,*
he and the dawn: *andante, ma non troppo.*
When I go to pick him up he is always standing,
as if the world needed a transfusion
and he is the only one with the right blood type.
I think it must be O. He *says* O.

The mockingbird will never earn a living,
not if he keeps this up. I want to tell him,
"Whatever the world means, it isn't simple.
Learn a trade. Think of the snapping turtle,
whose four hundred pounds per square inch of jaw
provides a firm grasp of the essentials."
But the mockingbird isn't big on survival.
He's just here, and keeps on noticing it.

2.

To become a father at forty-two is to know
a whole host of angular surprises
that somehow had escaped you. In the night
the least sounds announce *dispensable*,
and you wonder who they mean. The Muse, who up
till now has been voluptuous and kind,
begins to resemble your mother, or your wife,
who begins to resemble your Muse. It is most confusing.

You take to putting coasters under your drinks
and think that your wife's habit of clipping coupons
is perhaps not as nutty as you'd imagined.
You wink at the world, and the world says "Grow up!"
You thought that's what you were doing. But now machines,
which have always had the edge on you, are all
adding machines. Even the lawn mower,
and you have no lawn: you intended only to visit.

That's what you said. Now someone calls your bluff,
and you realize that that someone has your eyes
and probably isn't planning to give them back.
You try to think of what is important. Your life
has managed to follow you this far, sometimes close,
sometimes the way that dust is visible
and indicates a recent passerby
who must, it seems, be you; and is your father.

3.

Such fat discrepancies foil us all in time.
Too many choices, too many expectations.
Above the mockingbird's concatenations,
above the sound of distant railroad cars
uncoupling in the dark, above the rain
just beginning to fall, which is the sound
of my childhood in Seattle, something hums.
It made me think just now of '48.

and me alone in bed, home from school,
pretending to be sick, and the Baby Ben
humming its slow minutes, my mother gone—
shopping, I think—and the mirror starting to move,
and the sound of objects, falling throughout the house.
And that terrible sound from underneath, the earth
changing its mind. . . . But where I am now,
nothing moves but time. I'm sitting here,

the desk is solid oak, the typewriter
has interchangeable balls that stay in place
unless I decide to change them. The overhead
casts a consistent shadow, doesn't rise
or set, the rain keeps coming down, and the cat
hasn't moved for hours except to yawn.
And now and then the coupled freight cars pass
as if nothing has happened. And nothing has.

4.

Against the grain of any solid house
the world doesn't love us one by one.
I don't mean summer houses, of course, which hang
like the matter-at-hand above an argument
for spontaneous feelings, or houses that are rented
in cities or towns everywhere and that,
to nourishment, are like those catalogues
of daily minimum requirements.

I mean a house whose grace, conventional
or not, is adequate to the need for grace
and which, therefore, betokens a kind of freedom
for those who inhabit it, summer or winter—
a house, let's say, flanked by stentorian laurels.
Such a house survives in my body now.
Wherever I go, the compass point of caring
wavers toward that north, though where it stood

a freeway runs, and where the upstairs bedroom
window, once, looked out upon the slow
unfolding of hawthorne buds, or the Basil girls
sunbathing across the street, cars careen
toward Canada, or south, toward Oregon.
That house, I began to say, survives in my body
now, and nowhere else. Between our bodies
and the world, what barriers do we raise?

5.

These days a woman I love, a child I love
move the air of their lives from place to place
in little imperceptible shifts. Or else
one picks up an object and hands it to the other,
simply. Or else they are both asleep, as now,
and their breathing becomes the object one
gives to the air and the air gives to the other.
I think it is time to make my peace with objects,

whatever their practical use: ceramic cups
I keep my pencils in, if only because,
like all good reasons not to be alarmed,
they won't hold water; placemats macraméd
in adult education classes; little
magnets shaped like owls or bunnies, which,
placed on the refrigerator, slip
at the least touch of a shopping list. Because

when a child begins to walk, the furniture
grows new edges, hexagons from squares,
and knives hang from the usually peaceful plants.
While over in the corner a single object—
who knows which one?—rehearses its nomenclature
of "ball" or "train" or "duck," whereas till now
it has slept in its safe shape of wood or plastic,
happy and anonymous and whole.

6.

"Man gives proof of reflection," Herder writes,
"when out of the whole drifting dream of images
that passes by his senses he can collect,
in one moment of wakefulness, himself,
can pick out for himself characteristics
which show that this is the object, and no other."
Reflection, in other words, is one of the ways
by which we cheat the obvious of its power.

I don't mean to complain. It is all right.
But what is this need humming in the night
that is not my next-door neighbor's electric typewriter,
that is not insomnia taking a short stroll,
that is not the sex-life of teenagers, tuning up?
The earth, I think, is a curveball God is throwing
in slow motion and you and I are here
just as it leaves his hand. It is all right,

but what is this need humming in the night
that is not a total eclipse of the moon, just missing,
that is not the player piano of time, that is not
anything you or I will ever explain
although we undo ourselves line by line
until we are all paper, like a kite
some child has let slip. It is all right,
but what is this need humming in the night?

II. The First Morning of Fathers

1.

The first morning of fathers is horizontal:
it seems to go on forever. But that is because
the sky, like a mother with many children, has been
up the entire night, pressing it out.
On the Clackamas River Road the highway bends
at a clearing, and the river, which up till now
has been the highway's sibling, almost a twin,
looms like a train of thought that doesn't love us.

At just this place, perverse, I park my car,
exchange my boots for waders, don my vest-
of-the-many-pockets and, rod in hand,
head down to the river. It is morning:
at home a woman sleeps in our bed alone
dreaming of rivers with many rooms, while in
an adjoining room our one-year son begins
to nuzzle the world—the one he lets us use

when he's not using it. I think of him
as the current hugs my legs and holds on tight,
as if I were responsible. I think:
if love were enough, life would be too easy,
and make my first cast across the river,
and let the line drift down, and reel it in,
invisible almost, but in its way
the surest tie I have to anything.

2.

Birds on the river know who owns the morning.
Not the heron so much—there, downriver,
pretending to be a branch. You have to imagine
the sky cross-hatched by their flight-paths, thick or fine,
variegated, a web they go on stitching,
a safety net for the dead, to know what I mean.
Even wisdom gets boring. Even your own.
I have lived on this planet for more than forty years

and what do I know? There is a town called Boring,
Oregon, which has its beauty. There is
a town called Wisdom, Montana, where I have been.
The sound of the bus pulling into Wisdom
is the sound of the future snapping shut
its sample-case of alternatives. It is
the sound of all the decisions you never made
trying to talk at once, and being successful.

It is the sound of the last gunslinger, weeping.
Meanwhile, back in Boring, a baby is trying
hard to be born, his elongated head
just beginning to crown for the anxious doctor
and nurses, his lungs rehearsing their first scream
in a silence as dark as a gun-barrel. But here on the river,
morning—its matter-of-fact tenderness—breaks,
and the birds begin, again, to piece it together.

3.

The steelhead come back to the river. They are not salmon.
They are not swallows returning to Capistrano.
They are, as the guide books say, sea-going trout,
though they do not believe in guide books, or in the sea
with its loud need for approval, roaring like that.
They believe in the river, in a certain insistent urge
for which the river's a metaphor, but a good one.
They believe in this so firmly that there are people

who line the banks in cuneiforms of praise,
trying to make themselves invisible.
Somewhere else, on subways, invisible people
raise one arm like this; the subway tracks
run like a steel river under the city
and people rise early to line its banks, and the sound
that the subway makes is like the name of the river—
Clackamas. But I do not think it is praise.

I do not think the steelhead are fond of praise.
I do not seem to know what they are fond of.
The metaphors I offer them are not
the metaphors they want, or even good ones.
And yet the swallows, in spite of the tourists, return,
and the subway comes, and the steelhead mouths the lure
like an infant mouthing its first word, and you have
only an instant to set the hook. Hard.

4.

On the river, rain is a child practicing scales
who plays on the white keys only, except they are grey.
The child has not had lessons, and yet he knows
a scale when he hears one, and so he plays it over
and over: variations on a theme
without the variations. At forty-two
a man should know the real name for rain.
I've never understood how it comes down,

evaporates, and then comes down again.
Perhaps it doesn't. Perhaps we shouldn't believe
what we haven't seen; or perhaps we shouldn't believe
what we could see if a microscope decided
to prove it to us—that rain, for example, which seems
in our projected pain to be tear-shaped
really resembles little hamburger buns—
the last fast food, surely, this side of heaven.

At forty-two I'd rather believe that the river's
sentence goes on forever, and that the rain
and I are simply punctuation: upriver
the small parentheses of the drift I fish in
opens; downriver it closes. I'm here, a comma—
at most, a semicolon. Punctuation,
I like to tell my students, isn't important.
By which I mean: you should try to do it right.

5.

Although I know that words were never intended
to carry the weight of what we know, but like
the spider's filament were meant to catch,
intact, droplets of a mist through which
we call to one another for directions
precisely because we are not fish, or swallows—
in short, although I know it is unlikely,
I like to think the fish are waiting for words,

for something which, in my good moments, I could give them.
I think of the lovely fish, their silver sides,
their underbellies. Why should I deceive them?
Deception is not the point. I think of the fish
as balancing in the cool thought of the river,
moving for now neither forward nor backward,
but only waiting. I do not believe my lures,
why should the fish believe them? I do not believe

they will mistake me for heron or bear and be
afraid. I do not think they will mistake me
for brother or father and rush into my arms.
I think we are equals. I think that our balancing strengths
are like the thought of the river deep in the brain
of the fish, against which the fish, for now, move
neither forward nor backward, but hover, waiting,
perhaps for words, though I know it is unlikely.

6.

Driving home skunked, I think: *any problem*
that has an answer isn't important enough.
Coleridge knew: he woke one night—Hartley
asleep and Sara not yet born—and found
the windows flowered with frost, an analogue
of his mind's intricate beauty, hardening.
The French have a phrase for things you should have said
but think of only later: *thoughts of the stair*.

At Bonneville Dam steelhead are climbing the stairs
not thinking at all perhaps, though some of them stall,
like students lost for an answer, and never make it.
And then there's the soul's terrible climbing toward God.
And TV sets losing their vertical hold.
And my grandmother mounting the stairs of the nursing home
with the help of an aide who never watched her dance
to the tune of "Ragtime Cowboy Joe," her skirts

hiked modestly up and her five grandsons clapping.
As the fisherman said to the statistician, "Hell,
there ain't no average, it varies." Hitting the brake,
I swerve to avoid a dead raccoon on the road,
then turn off the windshield wipers. The sun is back,
like a lover who can't quite leave for good. The sky
is explaining this, and though I try hard to listen,
I really don't care. I need the world that much.

III. The Noon of Everything

1.

The sunflower, that baroque philosopher,
nods in the "west garden"—not that we have
an east or a north garden: it is a phrase
beloved of your mother, as is the flower,
which wakes each day, hefty and corrigible,
rendering her grandiloquent with praise.
Your mother is bilingual: she speaks love
in at least two tongues I can think of, fluently.

Once, on a field trip, she found a fish
gasping in a puddle on Sauvie Island.
Pregnant with you, she picked the damn thing up
and stumbled with it all the way to the lake.
The fish swam off—happy, your mother says.
An eagle, we conjectured, might have dropped it:
one eye was gone, one was all bloody.
We talked about it driving back. She said:

"Some sad things happen—even without man."
If no one knows they're sad, they're not sad,
I thought, but she was right, of course. That night,
I listened for your heartbeat with a glass.
Not finding it at first, I almost lied.
Then I found it. "Sounds just fine," I said.
She smiled her smile, and let it go at that.
Some happy things happen too. It evens out.

2.

The sunflower is a ball, which is to say
it is clearly not a dog, your other noun.
Placed above your reach, it verifies
that you are the issue here, like gravity.
The sun, its namesake, likewise is a ball
the dog day waits to chase, at your behest.
"Ball," you say. *"Doggy,"* you say. *"Papa?"*
"What?" I say. *"Lydle lydle lydle."*

You cultivate your words, your breath tending
each syllable, the way a man gone blind
might feel his way through a grove of rhododendrons.
Or the way that Galileo, old and blind,
puttered in his garden in Arcetri
after the Holy Office had made him promise
not to move the earth: a man of his word,
he couldn't resist, still, poking around.

A word, for you, is a happenstance of light,
a flower, which, if it's going to open at all,
opens when the world is paying attention
to something else, and then, some casual noon,
astounds the local inhabitants who pass,
reminded, for the moment, that (although
no truth can survive the blight of words)
things matter—some things more than others.

3.

The sunflower is conspicuously maned
and leonine. Amazed, I do not trust it.
A flower taller than me can mean no good,
and look: it sidles closer to the house
each day, it seems, frowsy with intent.
It signifies the noon of everything,
a time unloved by fishermen and poets,
as Van Gogh guessed: the flip side of despair.

Consider the docile springbok: when the buck
wishes to mate, he brushes the doe's flank
with one of his forelegs, as if asking permission—
what Chaucer meant, perhaps, by *gentilesse*.
The lion stalks the springbok. When he strikes,
the savannah shakes its dusty head like a man
startled momentarily from a nap,
and then, nothing amiss, nods off again.

Fishing is something else: only the fish
who decides to kill gets caught, a kind of justice.
Moreover, the fish has a fish-eye lens, which means
that riverbanks, the trees, the sky, myself,
surround the fish as the world surrounds a son
before he becomes a father: this, at bottom,
is what his existence means; he is the center.
Among the fish, there are no Galileos.

4.

When the springbok, locked in the lion's jaws,
knows he's the one, it makes him singular
in ways no human mind can ever imagine.
The other springbok, the zebras, the wildebeests,
watch from a safe distance, almost reverent.
Not that they learn. I don't believe they learn.
And what I say of the springbok—you have to think
past the unpleasantness of it, and the fear,

like a root-canal in the mind's eye. But it's there,
and the springbok knows: the thing about despair
is, it misses the point. No one deserves
anything. I tell you this because it is clear,
as few things are, and because whatever knowledge
we hope to live by winds back always
and eventually to just such stark beginnings.
The morning you were born, your mother's face

bore witness, as did yours, your crimped eyes
already edged with pain. Though the rules change,
though the thin chambers of our usual discourse
anticipate no realities which adhere,
I wish for you unshakeable faith in a wisdom
that will outlive the springbok or the lion,
you or me, my love for you, huge as it is,
and the air's apparent kindness as it kills.

5.

Nicolas, *Nikoláki mou*,
I'm trying to say a simple thing clearly.
Not "The sun again, with its long skein of laughter,"
nor "flowers that rise like apples at the sills
of all our windows," though they are real enough,
those flowers, that sun. Something about love,
I think, though love can be as scarce as money
and I never could tell decimal points from commas.

I do tell time, and yet it won't be long,
because of digital clocks, before the term
clockwise makes no sense, and this is sad:
even this minor wisdom, *tick* and *tock*,
is something we can hardly afford to lose.
A girl sits in her small room deciding
to cut her hair or not to cut her hair:
it is like that. It is that important.

And this is just one example. I think of the people
who started the great cathedral at Chartres, and the point
at which the stone took on its own—sublime,
perhaps, but also perverse—purpose, and they
trying to tell their children the name for this.
Nicolas, the little hand is on you.
And love, I think, is a blank page of forget
from which, still, a few names are missing.

6.

As sunlight will catch the round edge of an object—
a teacup, say—and eliminate contour and color,
anything the eye could fasten on
or name, is the way you laugh on the intake, happy,
one of God's attention-getting devices
that still works. In closing, I mention this,
as in a parade of elephants the last
should seem the happiest, and be remembered.

Your mother, once, at a pachydermless zoo
with a group of school kids, complained: "It's hard
for children not to see an elephant."
It was as if an angel had started discussing
baseball, and I, who understand baseball,
didn't know enough about angels
to keep up the conversation. *It's hard
for anyone.* I thought, but didn't say it.

I felt like that when you were in her womb
reluctant to come out, your speech refined
to an intricate combination of kicks, although
the meaning came through clear: you liked it in there.
Nicolas, we live in the world that is offered,
however hard it seems. If *forgive* is the right
word, I say "Learn to forgive the world"—
if *world* is the right word. I leave it to you.

72

Library of Congress
Cataloging in Publication Data
Miranda, Gary.
Grace period.
(Princeton series of contemporary poets)
I. Title.   II. Series.
PS3563.I69G7   1983   811'.54   82-61373
ISBN 0-691-06571-3
ISBN 0-691-01406-x (pbk.)